tee

S

A

t

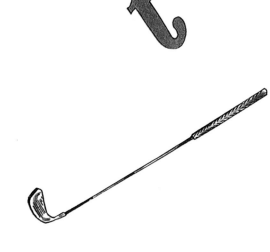

club

T

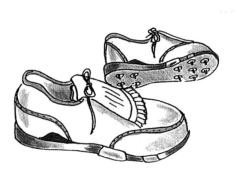

b

Swing easy,
stay positive
and have fun!

Susan
Greene

The ABC's of Golf

by Susan Greene
Illustrations by Nancy Bundorf

Excel Publishing, LLC
Troy, Michigan

It's fun to learn your ABC's
With golf balls, clubs, shoes and tees!

HOLE NO.9
PAR3
120 YARDS

A a

A hole in one

is for ace

s so much fun!

Bb is for ball

A golf ball is round,

With many a dimple,
But hitting it straight
Is not that simple.

C

C is for club

You need a club
To hit the ball,

But if you hit
Towards others,
"Fore"
Is your call.

D d is for dogleg

This golf hole is called
A **dogleg**.

Do you see why
Looking at
My dog
Meg?

E e is for electric cart

If you take an **electric** cart,
An adult should drive
Right from the start.

F f is for flagstick

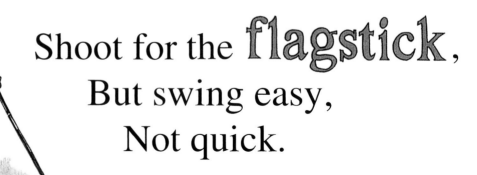

Shoot for the flagstick,
But swing easy,
Not quick.

Gg is for green

Green is more than a color
In the golf game.

Every green is different.
There aren't two the same.

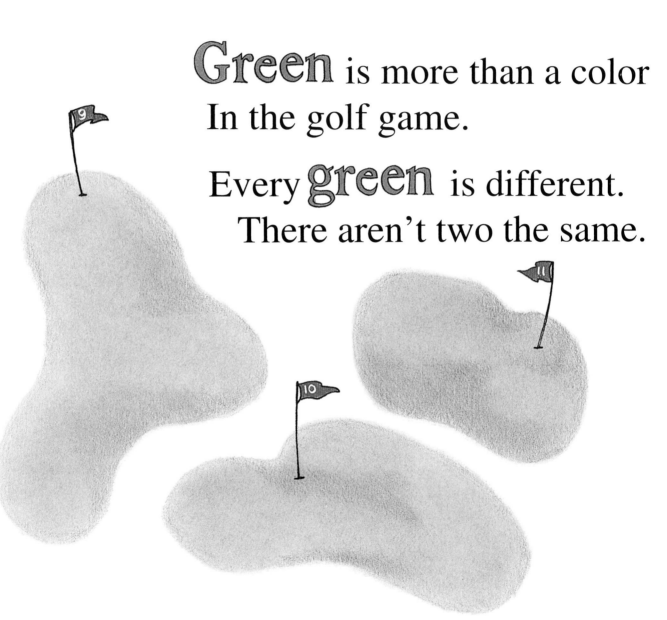

H h is for hands

Place your **hands**
Upon the club,
But not too tightly.
Grip it lightly!

I i is for instructor

See an **instructor** to improve,
And get your swing in a groove.

J j is for junior golf

Play **junior** golf
For some fun.
You can play it
In the sun.

K k is for keep score

HOLE NO.	1	2	3	4	5	6	7	8	9	10	11	12	13	14	15	16	17	18	TOTALS
You	3	4	5	3	6	5	7	4	3										
Me	4	3	5	2	5	6	4	7	5										
Friend	5	3	6	4	3	4	5	6	5										
Buddy	3	4	5	4	4	5	4	6	5										

THE HAVIN' FUN GOLF COURSE

1, 2, 3, 4 ...or 5?

Keep score
On every hole.

It is good
For your soul.

L₁ is for land

Keep the ball on dry land .
Avoid hazards,
Like water and sand.

M m

is for metal wood

I wouldn't think that they could.
Oh my gosh,
A metal wood!

N n is for nine holes

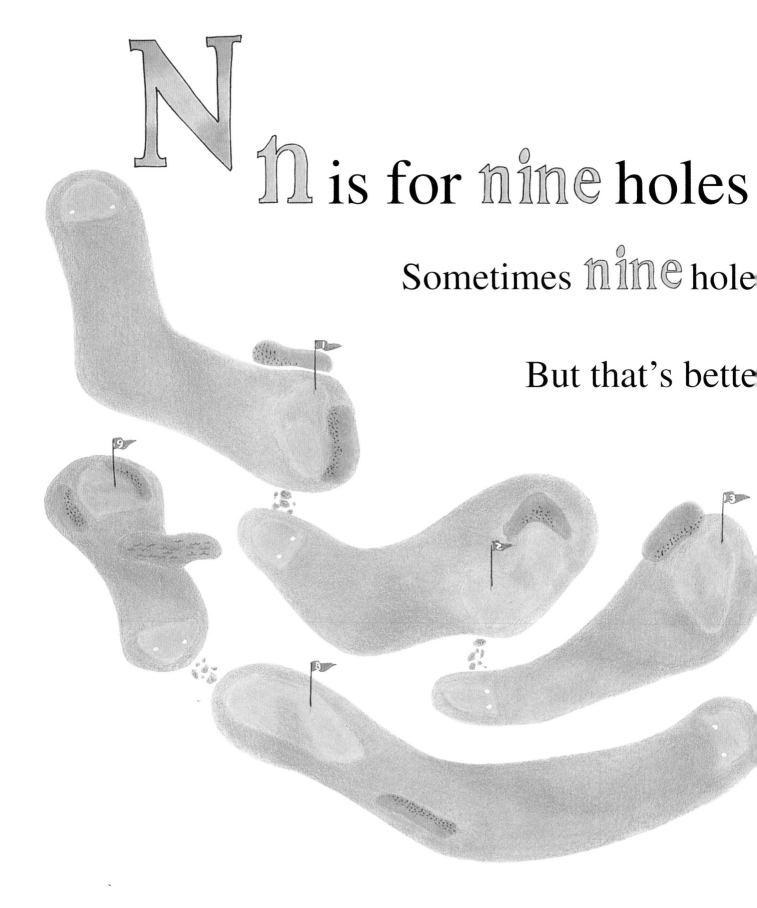

Sometimes nine hole

But that's bette

s all you can play,

nan not playing

At all that day.

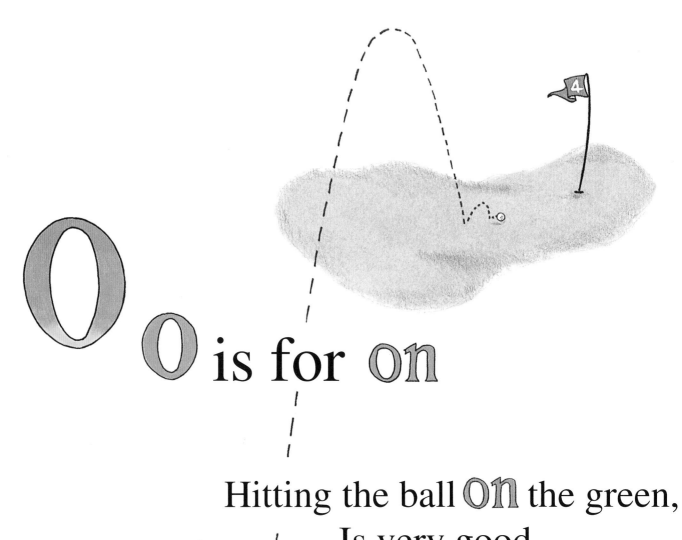

O o is for on

Hitting the ball **on** the green,
Is very good,
And part of the scene.

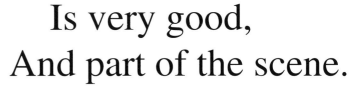

P p is for putting

But, **putting** the ball in the hole
Is the ultimate goal!

Q q is for quiet

There is no
If, and or but.

Remain quiet
While others putt.

R r is for rules

You must follow
The **rules** of the game,

Or you will be
Put to shame.

S s is for

shoes and spikes

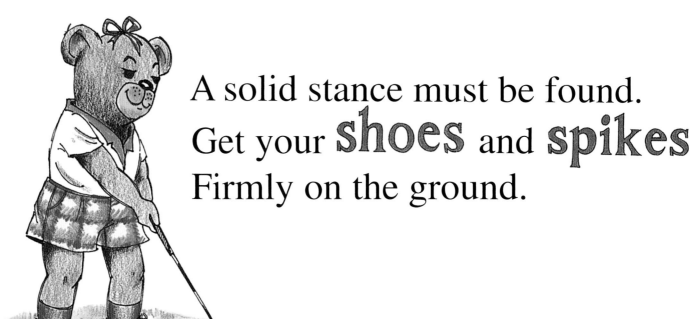

A solid stance must be found.
Get your **shoes** and **spikes**
Firmly on the ground.

T t is for tee

Start the game
With a **tee** .

Set your ball on it,
Then swing free.

U u is for umbrella

Since weather isn't always the same,
Carry an **umbrella**
And be ahead of the game.

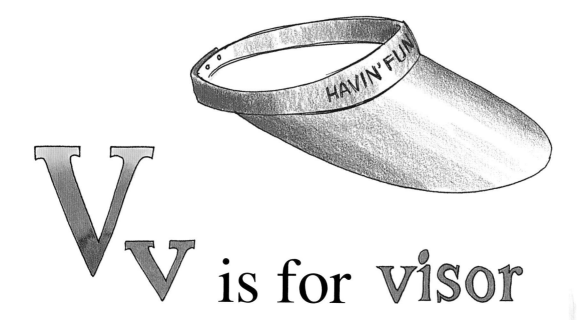

Vv is for visor

When the glare of the sun
Makes it hard to see,
Put on a visor
For a quick remedy.

Ww is for whiff

If you **whiff**,
Don't feel sad.

It's not really
All that bad.

Xx is for eXercise

EXercise before you play,
So your ball won't go astray.

Yy is for yardage markers

Hit the green,
If you can.

Yardage markers
Help you plan.

Z z is for zigzag

If you zigzag,
It's still fun.
You see more of the course
When it's all said and done.

To reinforce the alphabet,
We'll do a review.
Say the missing letters,
And we'll see how you do.
Look back through the pages,
If you need a clue!

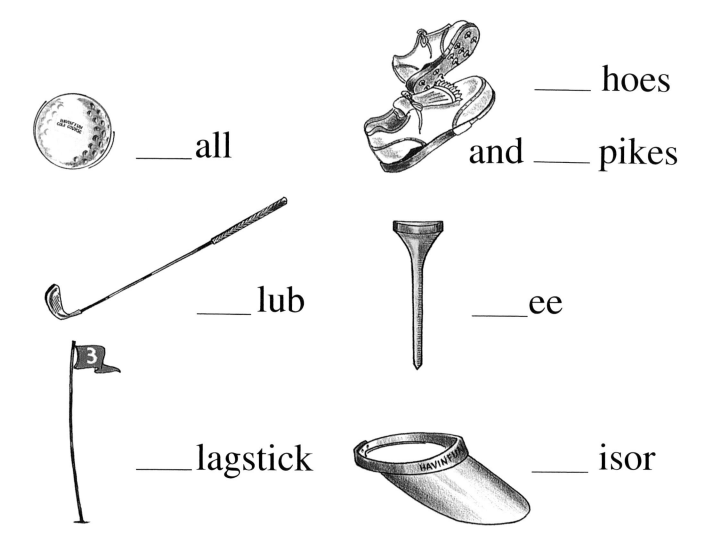

____ hoes

____all

and ____ pikes

____ lub

____ee

____lagstick

____ isor

The ABC's of Golf
Is a breeze.

From A to Z,
You learn with ease!

ball

shoes

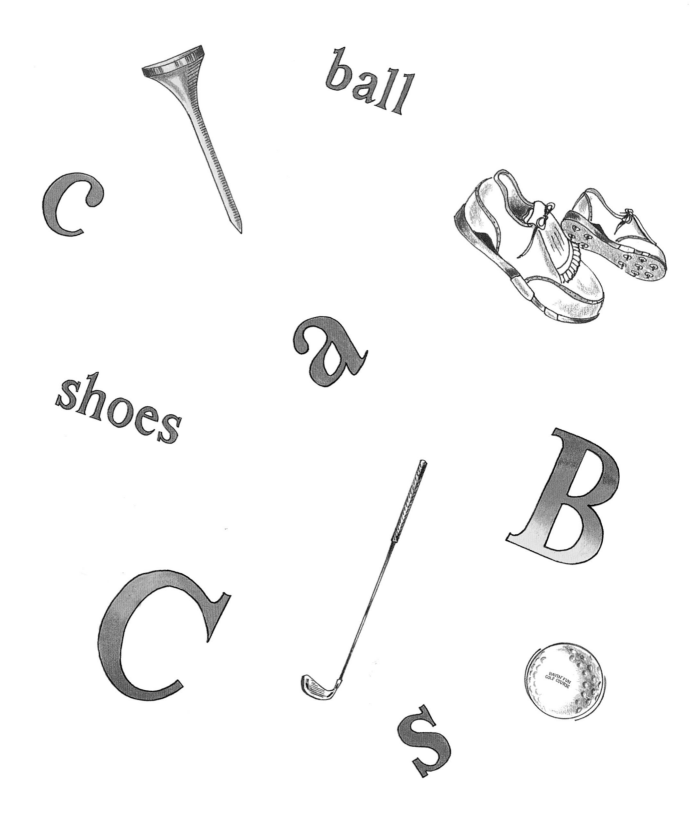